Also by Jorie Graham

HYBRIDS OF PLANTS AND OF GHOSTS

EROSION

REGION OF UNLIKENESS

MATERIALISM

THE DREAM OF THE UNIFIED FIELD: SELECTED POEMS 1974–1994

EARTH TOOK OF EARTH: 100 GREAT POEMS OF THE ENGLISH LANGUAGE, *Editor*

THE BEST AMERICAN POETRY 1990, *Editor*

THE ERRANCY

The End of Beauty

THE END OF BEAUTY

JORIE GRAHAM

THE ECCO PRESS

Copyright © 1987 by Jorie Graham
All rights reserved
The Ecco Press
100 West Broad Street
Hopewell, New Jersey 08525
Published simultaneously in Canada by
Penguin Books Canada Ltd., Ontario
Printed in the United States of America
Library of Congress Cataloging in Publication Data
Graham, Jorie, 1951–
The end of beauty.
(The American poetry series ; v. 33)
I. Title.   II. Series.
PS3557.R214E5   1987   811'.54   86-24204
ISBN 0-88001-129-7
0-88001-616-7 (paper)

Acknowledgment is made to the editors of the
following magazines in which these poems first
appeared: The American Poetry Review, Antæus,
The New Yorker, Poetry, Parnassus, The Paris Review,
The Denver Quarterly, Tendril.

Grateful thanks to the Guggenheim Foundation and
the National Endowment for the Arts for grants
that enabled me to complete this book.

Special thanks to Eric Fischl for permission to use a detail
from his painting "Untitled" (Two women in bedroom) on the cover.

9 8 7 6 5 4 3

FOR EMILY VAN-WANING GALVIN

CONTENTS

The End of Beauty

SELF-PORTRAIT
AS THE GESTURE BETWEEN THEM

[ADAM AND EVE]

1

The gesture like a fruit torn from a limb, torn swiftly.

2

The whole bough bending then springing back as if from sudden sight.

3

The rip in the fabric where the action begins, the opening of the narrow passage.

4

The passage along the arc of denouement once the plot has begun, like a limb,
the buds in it cinched and numbered,
outside the true story really, outside of improvisation,
moving along day by day into the sweet appointment.

5

But what else could they have done, these two, sick of beginning,
revolving in place like a thing seen,
dumb, blind, rooted in the eye that's watching,
ridden and ridden by that slowest of glances the passage of time
staring and staring until the entrails show.

6

Every now and then a quick rain for no reason,

7

a wind moving round all sides, a wind shaking the points of view out
like the last bits of rain. . . .

8

So it was to have freedom she did it but like a secret thought.
A thought of him the light couldn't touch.
The light beating against it, the light flaying her thought of him,
trying to break it.
Like a fruit that grows but only in the invisible.
The whole world of the given beating against this garden
where he walks slowly in the hands of freedom
noiselessly beating his steps against the soil.

9

But a secret grows, a secret wants to be given away.
For a long time it swells and stains its bearer with beauty.
It is what we see swelling forth making the shape we know a thing by.
The thing inside, the critique of the given.

1 0

So that she turned the thought of him in her narrow mind,
turned him slowly in the shallows, like a thin bird she'd found,
turned him in this place which was her own, as if to plant him but never
                                                    letting go,

keeping the thought of him keen and simple in a kind of winter,
keeping him in this shadowlessness in which he needn't breathe,
him turning to touch her as a thing turns towards its thief,
owned but not seizable, resembling, resembling. . . .

1 1

Meanwhile the heights of things were true. Meanwhile the distance of
the fields was true. Meanwhile the fretting of the light against the backs
                                                                    of them
as they walked through the fields naming things, true,
the touch of the light along the backs of their bodies . . .

1 2

as the apple builds inside the limb, as rain builds
in the atmosphere, as the lateness accumulates until it finally
is,
as the meaning of the story builds,

1 3

scribbling at the edges of her body until it must be told, be

1 4

taken from her, this freedom,

1 5

so that she had to turn and touch him to give it away

[5]

to have him pick it from her as the answer takes the question

that he should read in her the rigid inscription

in a scintillant fold the fabric of the daylight bending

where the form is complete where the thing must be torn off

momentarily angelic, the instant writhing into a shape,

the two wedded, the readyness and the instant,

the extra bit that shifts the scales the other way now in his hand,
the gift that changes the balance,

the balance that cannot be broken owned by the air until he touches,

24

the balance like an apple held up into the sunlight

25

then taken down, the air changing by its passage, the feeling of being capable,

26

of being not quite right for the place, not quite the thing that's needed,

27

the feeling of being a digression not the link in the argument,
a new direction, an offshoot, the limb going on elsewhere,

28

and liking that error, a feeling of being capable *because* an error,

29

of being wrong perhaps altogether wrong a piece from another set

30

stripped of position stripped of true function

31

and loving that error, loving that filial form, that break from perfection

3 2

where the complex mechanism fails, where the stranger appears in the cleari

3 3

out of nowhere and uncalled for, out of nowhere to share the day.

ON DIFFICULTY

It's that they want to know *whose* they are,
seen from above in the half burnt-out half blossomed-out
woods, late April, unsure as to whether to
turn back.
The woods are not their home.
The blossoming is not their home. Whatever's back there
is not. Something floats in the air all round them
as if *it* were the place
where the day drowns,
and the place at the edge of cries, for instance, that fissure, gleams.
Now he's holding his hand out.
Is there a hollow she's the shape of?
And in their temples a thrumming like
what-have-I-done?—but not yet a question, really, not
yet what slips free of the voice to float like a brackish foam
on emptiness—
Oh you will come to it, you two down there
where the vines begin, you will come to it,
the thing towards which you reason, the place where the flotsam
of the meanings is put down
and the shore
holds. They're thinking *we must have slept a while,*
what is it has changed? They're thinking
how low the bushes are, after all, how finite
the options one finds in the
waiting (after all). More like the branchings of whiteness
always stopping short into this shade or that,

breaking inertia then stopping,
breaking the current at last into shape but then
stopping—
If you asked them, where they first find the edges of each other's bodies, *wher*
happiness resides they'd look up through the gap
in the greenery you're looking down through.
What they want to know—the icons silent in the shut church (to the left),
the distance silent in the view (to the right)—
is how to give themselves *away*,
which is why they look up now,
which is why they'll touch each other now (for your
looking), which is why they want to know what this
reminds you of
looking up, reaching each other for you to see, for you to see by, the long sleep
beginning, the long sleep of resemblance,
touching each other further for you that Eternity begin, there, between you,
letting the short jabs of grass hold them up for you to count by,
to color the scene into the believable by,
letting the thousands of individual blossoms add up
and almost (touching her further) block your view of them—
When you look away
who will they be dear god and what?

DESCRIPTION

Meet me, meet me whisper the waters from the train window and the small
                                                                    skiff adrift
with its passenger, oarless, being pulled in by
some destination, delicate, a blossom on the wing of
the swollen waters.

Will you take him there to the remedy he needs, intelligence,
current, will you take him singing his song, back in, note by
note? She has the
antidote, the girl at the end, the girl who is the end, she has the only
      cure

which is her waiting and waiting, which is how she will not move or
                                                            change
her mind that is
no mind. Waste
and empty
      the sea,

love, through which the only passage tugs.
He's floating down through the air-killed reeds,
      past the refinery,
he's floating stretched out in that eye-shaped
boat (is he

awake?), the parking lot of the recycling plant
returning to the light

maybe a thousand bodies of cars, the argument
changing, changing,

till it's later and you can look
because the brightness has gone.
There's a church in back of which a parking lot
is weeds (the water is widening, will he

awaken?) and the flat tarred roof of the Martin
Marietta plant so thick with broken glass and ash at 97mph, the words LAST
                                                                    and ANITA
spelled out in empties

on one end. The tar
must be hot now I
think or he thinks floating under the rush hour traffic through the
                                                        cooler bands
under the bridge, his tiny craft

blinking on and off where patches of glass still hold
in the corners of the gutted
        warehouse windows,
a bit of him quick
in each splinter,
        unseized, unatoned, his passage helplessly re-

iterated, stuttered and finally extinguished where the buildings end
                                                and the oilfields
begin. The cemetery; the demolition
yard; someone's gigantic crane
sorting soft metals from hard from plastic from

glass into beautiful
mounds. He's almost

at the mouth now. Will I see him awaken? Will I
    see him
go under, the highways thicker here, the sound of speed

overriding the winds? The reasons
for things, love, are growing
wild; wild and inaudible in these meadows of lateness.
The *reasons* sticky like hot light over all

the combustible fluids—: still apart, spark and fuel,
still bodied, still free. Westward strain the eyes,
eastward the ship flies, the rudderless boat, the sleepy
passenger mortally

wounded. How far will he go pulled in by the listening of that far
                                                    shore?
And as she approached, unable still to see any body
    within,
she heard to her heart's delight a lovely harp,
    a sweet voice,
and as long as he harped and as long as he sang
    she never stirred to

save him.

SELF-PORTRAIT
AS BOTH PARTIES

1

The cut flowers riding the skin of this river.

2

Dallying, dallying, wanting to go in.

3

Wanting to be true, at the heart of things but true.

4

Imagine the silt and all that it was.
The grains that filter down to it through the open hands of the sunlight.
How its rays weaken down there. How when it comes to touch
that smoothest of girls the slow bottom of the river,
is it Orpheus as it glides on unharmed but really
turned back with its one long note that cannot
break down?

5

How would he bring her back again? She drifts up
in a small hourglass-shaped cloud of silt where the sunlight touches,
up to where the current could take her,

up by the waist into the downstream motion again into the
hard sell, and for a moment even I can see
the garment of particles which would become her body,
swaying, almost within reason, this devil-of-the-bottom,
almost yoked again, almost quelling her weightlessness,
flirting here now with this handful of
mudfish his fingers touch silver. . . . But they gun

6

through the weeds, the weeds cannot hold her
who is all rancor, all valves now, all destination,
dizzy with wanting to sink back in,
thinning terribly in the holy separateness.
And though he would hold her up, this light all open hands,
seeking her edges, seeking to make her palpable again,
curling around her to find crevices by which to carry her up,
flaws by which to be himself arrested and made,
made whole, made sharp and limbed, a shape,
she cannot, the drowning is too kind,
the becoming of everything which each pore opens to again,
the possible which each momentary outline blurs into again,
too kind, too endlessly kind,
the silks of the bottom rubbing their vague hands
over her forehead, braiding her to

7

the sepulchral leisure, the body, the other place that is not minutes

8

from which he searches he searches which is his majesty

all description all delay this roundabout the eye must love.

ORPHEUS AND EURYDICE

Up ahead, I know, he felt it stirring in himself already, the glance,
the darting thing in the pile of rocks,

already in him, there, shiny in the rubble, hissing Did you want to remain
completely unharmed?—

the point-of-view darting in him, shiny head in the ash-heap,

hissing Once upon a time, and then Turn now darling give me that look,

that perfect shot, give me that place where I'm erased. . . .

The thing, he must have wondered, could it be put to rest, there, in the
                                                                    glance,
could it lie back down into the dustyness, giving its outline up?

When we turn to them—limbs, fields, expanses of dust called meadow and
                                                                    avenue—
will they be freed then to slip back in?

Because you see he could not be married to it anymore, this field with
                                                        minutes in it
called woman, its presence in him the thing called

future—could not be married to it anymore, expanse tugging his mind out
                                                        into it,
tugging the wanting-to-finish out.

What he dreamed of was this road (as he walked on it), this dustyness,
but without their steps on it, their prints, without
song—

What she dreamed, as she watched him turning with the bend in the road
                                                                (can you
understand this?)—what she dreamed

was of disappearing into the seen

not of disappearing, lord, into the real—

And yes she could feel it in him already, up ahead, that wanting-to-turn-and-
cast-the-outline-over-her

by his glance,

sealing the edges down,

saying I know you from somewhere darling, don't I,
saying You're the kind of woman who etcetera—

(Now the cypress are swaying) (Now the lake in the distance)
(Now the view-from-above, the aerial attack of *do you
remember?*)—

now the glance reaching her shoreline wanting only to be recalled,
now the glance reaching her shoreline wanting only to be taken in,

(somewhere the castle above the river)

(somewhere you holding this piece of paper)

(what will you do next?) (—feel it beginning?)

now she's raising her eyes, as if pulled from above,

now she's looking back into it, into the poison the beginning,

giving herself to it, looking back into the eyes,

feeling the dry soft grass beneath her feet for the first time now the mind

looking into that which sets the _____ in motion and seeing in there

a doorway open nothing on either side
(a slight wind now around them, three notes from up the hill)

through which morning creeps and the first true notes—

For they were deep in the earth and what is possible swiftly took hold.

EXPULSION

In the cab, light plays down his neck from behind
making the collar shine, making his lifted fingers describe
something inhuman
even though they only meant to indicate
emphasis or touch the
glass divider. Once
the light seems to let his whole hand come to
the very edge of the burning
field. She thinks he touched her with it once
but can't recall. Did he? Were they nearing
their address? Cloud-cover gathered. At the studio, John
showed them two different prints of the Bresson
in which a figure seen from behind is running up
—or is it *into?*—an incandescent village (Greece), walls gone,
difference gone, shine, shine,
and then three windows and the one black door
that cut the light
making it come
true—Oh it's a city. And there are stairs. And there's
a girl about to
disappear.
According to which print you see, she's running towards something
or desperately away.
When greys govern it looks like fate, what holds the white
place down—
(barely)—
In the high-contrast print it looks like history—

They say this to each other holding one print in either
hand,
and then the photograph of Moore a week before she died,
then Faulkner looking away, back to the snarling dogs.
I think we misunderstand the Hopi injunction
against the photograph.
It's not that it steals the soul away.
Rather that *being-seen* will activate that soul,
until the flesh is something that can be risen through,
until the face you offer up is the one that can't be
helped.
Give me that look that says you know I'm seeing you but you
don't care, John said, sit still, yes
that's the look now, yes, that's
beautiful.
What was it she wanted to tell him
about the light as they left,
light coming to do what can be done
to hold a city?
Brick, glass, she might have whispered,
it slips in gratitude off of the wires he would have
said,
they cannot hold it, it loves them best—
Reader,
now it's almost visible to them, the *after wards,*
the face of the god who wouldn't be seen except from behind,
hand on his piece of rock,
hand pressing down where the young man hides.
What can you find looking up from this white page now,
what can you find across the room? Or is it a store? An
avenue?—See how they glow even now these minutes, this hiding
place—
Lord what were they meant to have done with it (shine, shine)—?

To take it up entire into themselves? extinguish it?
sucking the whole field up into the
present tense, turning each thing again and again
in their hands as if to see it *from all sides at once,* that
dream—
the visible having stood still for them for over a thousand
years whispering *describe,* whispering *take me*
back in—?
Isn't that what place had wanted
them for?

TO THE READER

I swear to you she wanted back into the shut, the slow,

a ground onto which to say This is my actual life, Good Morning,
onto which to say That girl on her knees who is me
is still digging that square yard of land up
to catalogue and press onto the page *all she could find in it*
and name, somewhere late April, where they believe in ideas,
Thursday, a little of what persists and all the rest.

Before that, dreams. The dream of being warm
and staying warm. The dream of the upper hand like a love song,
the dream of the right weapon and then the perfect escape.

Then the dream of the song of having *business* here.

Then the dream of you two sitting on the couch, of the mood
of armies (hand of God), of the city burning in the distance.

The dream of before and after (are we getting closer?) the dream
of *finally after days*. . . .

(Miss _____ lets out a shattering scream.)

I swear to you this begins with that girl on a day after sudden rain
and then out of nowhere sun (as if to expose *what* of the hills—
the white glare of x, the scathing splendor of y,
the wailing interminable _____?) that girl having run

down from the house and up over the fence not like an animal
but like a thinking, link by link, and over

into the allotted earth—for Science Fair—into the *everything* of
one square yard of earth. Here it begins
to slip. She took the spade and drew the lines. Right through
the weedbeds, lichen, moss, keeping the halves of things that landed *in*
by chance, new leaves, riffraff the wind blew in—

Here is the smell of earth being cut, the smell of the four lines.
Here is the brownsweet of the abstract where her four small furrows
say the one word over.
She will take the ruler and push it down till it's all the way in.
She will slide its razor edge along through colonies, tunnels,
through powdered rock and powdered leaf,

and everything on its way to the one right destination
like a cloak coming off, shoulders rising,
(after one has abandoned the idea of x;
after one has accorded to the reader the y)—
her hole in the loam like a saying in the midst of the field of patience,
fattening the air above it with detail,
an embellishment on the April air,
the rendezvous of hands and earth—

Say we leave her there, squatting down, haunches up,
pulling the weeds up with tweezers,
pulling the thriving apart into the true,
each seedpod each worm on the way down retrieved into a
plastic bag (shall I compare thee), Say we

leave her there, where else is there to go? A word,
a mouth over water? Is there somewhere

neither there nor here?
Where do we continue living now, in what terrain?
Mud, ash, _____, _____. We want it to stick to us,
hands not full but not clean. What is wide-meshed enough
yet lets nothing through, the bunch of ribbon,
her hair tied up that the wind be seen?

If, for instance, this was the place instead,

where the gods fought the giants and monsters
(us the ideal countryside, flesh, interpretation),

if, for instance, this were not a chosen place but a place
blundered into, a place which is a meadow with a hole in it,

and some crawl through such a hole to the other place

and some use it to count with and buy with

and some hide in it and see Him go by

and to some it is the hole on the back of the man running

through which what's coming towards him is coming into him, growing larger,

a hole in his chest through which the trees in the distance are seen
growing larger shoving out sky shoving out storyline

until it's close it's all you can see this moment this hole in his back

in which now a girl with a weed and a notebook appears.

WHAT THE END IS FOR

A boy just like you took me out to see them,
    the five hundred B-52's on alert on the runway,
fully loaded fully manned pointed in all the directions,
    running every minute
of every day.
    They sound like a sickness of the inner ear,

where the heard foams up into the noise of listening,
    where the listening arrives without being extinguished.
The huge hum soaks up into the dusk.
    The minutes spring open. Six is too many.
From where we watch,
    from where even watching is an anachronism,

from the 23rd of March from an open meadow,
    the concertina wire in its double helix
designed to tighten round a body if it turns
    is the last path the sun can find to take out,
each barb flaring gold like a braille being read,
    then off with its knowledge and the sun
is gone. . . .

That's when the lights on all the extremities, like an outline like a dress,
    become loud in the story,
and a dark I have not seen before

sinks in to hold them one
by one.
     Strange plot made to hold so many inexhaustible
screams.
     Have you ever heard in a crowd mutterings of
blame

that will not modulate that will not rise?
     He tells me, your stand-in, they *stair-step* up.
He touches me to have me look more deeply
          in
to where for just a moment longer
          color still lives:
the belly white so that it looks like sky, the top
          some kind of brown, some soil—How does it look

from up there now
          this meadow we lie on our bellies in, this field Iconography
tells me stands for sadness
          because the wind can move through it uninterrupted?
What is it the wind
          would have wanted to find and didn't

leafing down through this endless admiration unbroken
          because we're too low for it
to find us?
     Are you still there for me now in that dark
we stood in for hours
          letting it sweep as far as it could down over us
unwilling to move, irreconcilable? What *he*
          wants to tell me,

his whisper more like a scream
     over this eternity of engines never not running,
is everything: how the crews assigned to each plane
     for a week at a time, the seven boys, must live
inseparable,
     how they stay together for life,
how the wings are given a life of
     seven feet of play,

how they drop practice bombs called *shapes* over Nevada,
     how the measures for counterattack in air
have changed and we
     now forego firepower for jamming, for the throwing
of false signals. The meadow, the meadow hums, love, with the planes,
     as if every last blade of grass were wholly possessed

by this practice, wholly prepared. The last time I saw you,
     we stood facing each other as dusk came on.
I leaned against the refrigerator, you leaned against the door.
     The picture window behind you was slowly extinguished,
the tree went out, the two birdfeeders, the metal braces on them.
     The light itself took a long time,

bits in puddles stuck like the useless
     splinters of memory, the chips
of history, hopes, laws handed down. *Here, hold these* he says, these
     grasses these
torn pods, he says, smiling over the noise another noise, *take these*
     he says, my hands wrong for

the purpose, here,
     not-visible-from-the-sky, prepare yourself with these, boy and
bouquet of

thistleweed and wort and william and
timothy. We stood there. Your face went out a long time
　　　before the rest of it. Can't see you anymore I said. *Nor I,
you, whatever you still were*
　　　replied.
When I asked you to hold me you refused.
　　　When I asked you to cross the six feet of room to hold me

you refused. Until I
　　　couldn't rise out of the patience either any longer
to make us
　　　take possession.
Until we were what we must have wanted to be:
　　　shapes the shapelessness was taking back.
Why should I lean out?
　　　Why should I move?
When the Maenads tear Orpheus limb from limb,
　　　they throw his head

out into the river.
　　　Unbodied it sings
all the way downstream, all the way to the single ocean,
　　　head floating in current downriver singing,
until the sound of the cataracts grows,
　　　until the sound of the open ocean grows and the voice.

SELF-PORTRAIT
AS APOLLO AND DAPHNE

1

The truth is this had been going on for a long time during which
    they both wanted it to last.

You can still hear them in that phase, the north and
south laid up against each other, constantly erasing
each minute with each minute.

You can still hear them, there, just prior to daybreak,
the shrill cheeps and screeches of the awakening thousands,
hysterical, for miles, in all the directions,

and there the whoo whoo of the nightfeeders, insolvent baseline,
shorn, almost the sound of thin air. . . .

Or there where the sun picks up on the bits of broken glass
throughout the miles of grass for just a fraction of an instant
(thousands of bits) at just one angle, quick, the evidence,
    the landfill,
then gone again, everything green, green. . . .

2

How he wanted, though, to possess her, to nail the erasures,

3

like a long heat on her all day once the daysounds set in, like
a long analysis.

4

The way she kept slipping away was this: can you really
see me, can you really know I'm really who . . .
His touchings a rhyme she kept interrupting (no one
believes in that version anymore she whispered, no one
can hear it anymore, *tomorrow, tomorrow,*
like the different names of those girls
all one girl). . . . But how long could it
last?

5

He kept after her like sunlight (it's not what you think, she said)
frame after frame of it (it's not what you think you think)
like the prayer that numbers are praying (are they ascending are they
descending?)

He kept after her in the guise of the present,
minute after minute (are they ascending are they?)
until they seemed to quicken and narrow (like footprints

piling up, like footprints all blurred at the end of, at the scene of . . .)

until *now is forever* he whispered can't you get it to open,

present tense without end, slaughtered motion, kingdom of
heaven?—

6

the shards caught here and there—*what did you do
before?* or *will you forgive me?* or *say
that you'll love me for*

ever and ever

(is it a squeal of brakes is it a birthcry?)

(let x equal forever he whispered let y let y . . .)

7

as opposed to that other motion which reads Cast it upon the ground
and it shall become a serpent (and Moses fled before it),
which reads Put forth thy hand and take it by the tail
and it was a rod in his hand again—

8

That's when she stopped, she turned her face to the wind, shut her eyes—

9

She stopped she turned,
she would not be the end towards which he was ceaselessly tending,
she would not give shape to his hurry by being
        its destination,
it was wrong this progress, it was a quick iridescence
on the back of some other thing, unimaginable, a flash on the wing of . . .

10

The sun would rise and the mind would rise
and the will would rise and the eyes—The eyes—:
the whole of the story like a transcript of sight,
of the distance between them, the small gap he would close.

11

She would stop, there would be no chase scene, she would
    be who,
what?

12

The counting went on all round like a thousand birds
each making its own wind—who would ever add them up?—

and what would the sum become, of these minutes, each flapping
its wings, each after a perch,

each one with its call going unanswered,

each one signaling separately into the end of the daybreak,

the great screech of the instants, the pile-up,
the one math of hope, the prayer nowhere is praying,

frame after frame, collision of tomorrows—

No she would go under, she would leave him in the freedom

his autograph all over it, slipping, trying to notch it,

1 3

there in the day with him now, his day, but altered,

1 4

part of the view not one of the actors, she thought,

not one of the instances, not one of the examples,

1 5

but the air the birds call in,
the air their calls going unanswered marry in,
the calls the different species make, cross-currents, frettings,
and the one air holding the screeching separateness—
each wanting to change, to be heard, to have been changed—
and the air all round them neither full nor empty,
but holding them, holding them, untouched, untransformed.

ESCHATOLOGICAL PRAYER

In Montefalco, Italy,
    late in the second millennium
of a motion measured
    by its distance from the death
of a single young man,

we drove up a narrow road cut like a birthcry
    into the hillside, winding and twisting
up to the top.
    Snow gleamed in the margins, originless.
Snow gleamed in the miles of birdcry and birdsong,

yellow birdsong in the yellow light.
    And the things of this world were everywhere happy
to be so grazed
    on only one side
by the fierce clean light

and by us
    sifting the minutes from the dust from those three
almost repeatable
    notes
on which the whole unhearable song

depends.
    This is what time
as we knew it

was. You could reach almost in
to where the notes and the minutes

would touch.
        You could push. It was tenderness.
You could live in that gap, that listening.
        You could enter into that rock
and hide thee in that dust.
        Below us, appearing and re-

appearing,
        the airplane factory now closed and converted
into a temporary
        slaughterhouse—
no sound from there just now,
        the wind being against us,

and the turning and the winding
        upward. To whom it may concern,
we were a people
        to cut such roads
up through the middle of a valley,

a road like the dream of a perfect
        calculation, a sum so accurate
it bursts,
        up through a greenery,
up, if you must know,
        for the anger, for the view

from above.
        For you who must know,

for you, imaginary
        destination, quick
young god; for the end of
        the story
listening and listening now as it pulls us on
        in: in the church

of Santa Chiara
        di Montefalco
you could in early 1985 by a door to the left
        of the main altar
pull
        a chain that titters a distant bell
until a woman
        who has paid her body out for this life to waiting

        presses her beautiful nowhere
against the face-sized grille repeated speech
        has oxidized green
about the mouth.
        She will ask you what it is you
wish.
        You say you've come to see

the saint.
        Maybe she asks you if you have come from
far away. Maybe there is an old woman
        sobbing in the aisles between the two
altars, maybe she bends over to kiss the lung-colored holywater
        and you can see the spot
where her thick black stockings stop
        above her knees in wide

elastic bands as I did,
    maybe you watch her turn away as if parched
from the girl in the shimmering glass casket
    lights have suddenly
spit up for us,

this Claire who saw the god in 1300 drop
    under the weight of his cross
and swore to carry it
    forever in her heart.
They cut her open when she died, the sisters prying
    between the curtains of light and the curtains

of light. They found in there,
    in the human heart,
this tiny crucifix, this eye-sized figure
    of tissue and blood.
Here are the penknife, the scissors. Here are the towels
    they soaked the blood

up into, here the three kidney stones, the piece
    of lung in the shape
of a bird, here the story the hurry like so and like
    so, and the singing voices now that it's noon
of the cloistered sisters
    back in there barely audible so clean like acetylene

as if they were biting
    down onto the light. Whatever it is we must hurry
into,
    we were a motion that judged difference
and loved it
    and wanted to take it

into our bodies,
    a motion that wanted to splinter
all the way open yet still
    be,
a stirring that wanted to be expected
    somewhere yet

still be,
    that wanted syllable by syllable to be shattered
over the whole of eternity
    into the eyes into the mouths of strangers yet still be,
words bones bits the whole
    franchisement
glances promises

and still be.

NOLI ME TANGERE

You see the angels have come to sit on the delay
    for a while,
they have come to harrow the fixities, the sharp edges
    of this open
sepulcher,
    they have brought their swiftnesses like musics

down
    to fit them on the listening.
Their robes, their white openmindedness gliding into the corners,
    slipping this way then that
over the degrees, over the marble

flutings.
    The small angelic scripts pressing up through the veils.
The made shape pressing
    up through the windy cloth.
I've watched all afternoon how the large
    red birds here

cross and recross neither for play nor hunger
    the gaps that constitute our chainlink fence,
pressing themselves narrowly against the metal,
    feeding their bodies and wings

tightly in.
        Out of what ceases into what is ceasing.
Out of the light which holds steel and its alloys,

into the words for it like some robe or glory,
        and all of this rising up into the deep unbearable thinness,
the great babyblue exhalation of the one God
        as if in satisfaction at some right ending
come,

then down onto the dustyness that still somehow holds
        its form as downslope and new green meadow
through which at any moment
        something swifter
might cut.
        It is about to be
Spring.
        The secret cannot be

kept.
        It wants to cross over, it wants
to be a lie.

2

Is that it then? Is that the law of freedom?
        That she must see him yet must not touch?
Below them the soldiers sleep their pure deep sleep.
        Is he light
who has turned forbidding and thrust his hand up
        in fury,

is he flesh
　　so desperate to escape, to carry his purpose away?
She wants to put her hands in,
　　she wants to touch him.
He wants her to believe,
　　who has just trusted what her eyes have given her,

he wants her to look away.
　　I've listened where the words and the minutes would touch,
I've tried to hear in that slippage what
　　beauty is——
her soil, his sweet tune like footsteps
　　over the path of

least resistance. I can see
　　the body composed
of the distance between them.
　　I know it is ours: he must change, she must
remember.
　　But you see it is not clear to me why she

must be driven back,
　　why it is the whole darkness that belongs to her
and its days,
　　why it is these hillsides she must become,
supporting even now the whole weight of the weightless,
　　letting the plotlines wander all over her,

crumbling into every digressive beauty,
　　her longings all stitchwork towards his immaculate rent,
all alphabet on the wind as she rises from prayer. . . .

3

It is the horror, Destination,
    pulling the whole long song
down, like a bad toss
    let go
in order to start again right,
    and it is wrong

to let its one inaudible note govern our going
    isn't it, siren over this open meadow
singing always your one song of shape of
    home. I have seen how the smoke here
inhabits a space
    in the body of air it must therefore displace,

and the tree-shaped gap the tree inhabits,
    and the tree-shaped gap the tree
invents. Siren,
    reader,
it is here, only here,
    in this gap

between us,
    that the body of who we are
to have been
    emerges: imagine:
she lets him go,
    she lets him through the day faster than the day,

among the brisk wings
    upsetting the flowerpots,
among the birds arranging and rearranging the shape of

the delay,
she lets him
       slip free,

letting him posit the sweet appointment,
       letting out that gold thread that crazy melody
of stations,
       reds, birds, dayfall, screen-door,
desire,

until you have to go with him, don't you,

until you have to leave her be
       if all you have to touch her with
is form.

T H E   V E I L

In the Tabernacle the veil hangs which is (choose one):
the dress dividing us from _____; the sky; the real,
through which the x ascends (His feet still showing through on
                                                  this side)
into the realm of uncreated things,
up, swift as proof,
leaving behind this *red* over our row of poplars now,
then just the poplars
a while longer,
then what we know as *gone*—the sky brightest for an instant
where a single motorcycle sputters
backfiring once.
Why this sudden silence?
What is the street, the time of day?
What is that young kid cruising towards against such minutes?
And the first person is where, please, in this place, pushing
      and watching?
Will the windows remain open much longer?
Will the mention of death occur even if only
once? And the cramped orchard of seven trees, soot-burnt,
above the traintracks, will it come to
stand for loss or only how knowledge lingers
against the linear? A train can be heard
(there is distance), and a voice calling an *Andrew* in
because the dampness, yes, is setting in and because no matter what
I'd do, unfinishing, the damp—as soon as sunlight's
gone—has rights in the matter even the author does not have

and the mother, calling and calling, knows this
who has been reading the same page over and over
                                        all afternoon
in her kitchen until it's darker than she thought
and still she won't get up.
Oh but you've seen her before, haven't you,
sitting at the table letting dusk come on,
unable to rise, flick the switch, let the new version
in.
It's that she wants to be free.
It's that she wants to be something the day must cross
not someone left to cross the day
along with the rest of the things.
Andrew is elsewhere (not even here). Andrew
is letting himself slip again and again
over a slick downleaning patch of moss the hill above the traintracks
owns. When he puts his hands in it he knows what
a *version* is, although he'd say to you, approaching in the evening,
that it *feels good* as the beginning of a story
feels good
just where it starts to freeze against the banks of
what it's not—
You see, there *is* a veil, or no, there is no veil but
there is
a rip in the veil,
which is the storyline,
what the lips just inconceivably apart can make
that cannot then, ever again, be uncreated—
(and then she wept) (and then a second backfire now at x remove)—
On the one side the tearing (the story)
on the other the torn (what it lets shine
through) and in between the veil being rent (*for all
eternity*) by this place made of words,

the gap her calling
would extinguish,
the mother of this story
—Because you see she is still calling,
bless her, she has an appointment for you to keep
and an indoors in which to keep it,
a stillness of place and circumstance which begins
when the lights go on and questions for which there is no answer
are asked out of kindness
and *love*—which is the stillest motion gets,
which is what description is as it reaches a listener,
love, in which the room is airy and light and open against change,
in which the room is exactly what you meant to say
(while across the street of course. . . .) (I'm writing this now lying
                                                        down, I'm

writing this now
into the mirror—can I take it from you, what would it take?)
love which is the mother calling you in and you going
so that this can have really happened and you
not know of the afternoon, for example, darkening where she read
the same page over and over for no reason,
the nothing-but-life sticky all over the walls,
the nothing-on-the-page swallowing the walls and so on
next to the photograph of her next to the fountain once—
You running up the stairs now into her
Good Evening Darling like an idea come back to life
where the ink dries, the body disappears, one more chair
is added,
you rushing in to be a point of view, wanting to live more deeply from
                                                        now on,

to live somewhere *else*,
though not yet (dear x) not yet—

SELF-PORTRAIT
AS HURRY AND DELAY

[PENELOPE AT HER LOOM]

1

So that every night above them in her chambers she unweaves it.
Every night by torchlight under the flitting shadows the postponement,
working her fingers into the secret place, the place of what is coming
    undone,

2

to make them want her more richly, there, where the pattern softens now,
    loosening,

3

to see what was healed under there by the story when it lifts,
by color and progress and motive when they lift,

4

the bandage the history gone into thin air,

5

to have them for an instant in her hands both at once,
the story and its undoing, the days the kings and the soil they're groundcover
    for

6

all winter,

7

against choice against offspring against the minutes like turrets
building the walls, the here and the there, in which he wanders searching,

8

till it lifts and the mouth of something fangs open there,
and the done and the undone rush into each other's arms.
A *mouth* or a gap in the fleshy air, a place in both worlds.
A woman's body, a spot where a story now gone has ridden.
The yarn springing free.
The opening trembling, the nothing, the nothing with use in it trembling—

9

Oh but is it wide enough to live on, immaculate present tense, lull
     between wars,

1 0

the threads running forwards yet backwards over her stilled fingers,

1 1

the limbs of the evergreens against the windowpane, the thousand hands,
beating then touching then suddenly still for no reason?

Reader, minutes:

now her fingers dart like his hurry darts over this openness he can't
    find the edge of,
like the light over the water seeking the place on the water
where out of air and point-of-view and roiling wavetips a shapeliness,
    a possession of happiness
forms,

a body of choices among the waves, a strictness among them, an edge
    to the light,

something that is not something else,

until she knows he's here who wants to be trapped in here,
her hands tacking his quickness down as if soothing it to sleep,
the threads carrying the quickness in on their backs,
burying it back into there, into the pattern, the noble design,
like a stain they carry past a sleeping giant,
the possible like kindling riding in on their backs,
the flames enlarging and gathering on the walls,
wanting to be narrowed, rescued, into a story again, a transparence we
can't see through, a lover

1 5

approaching ever approaching the unmade beneath him,
knotting and clasping it within his motions,
wrapping himself plot plot and dénouement over the roiling openness. . . .

1 6

Yet what would she have if he were to arrive?
Sitting enthroned what would either have?
It is his wanting in the threads she has to keep alive for him,
scissoring and spinning and pulling the long minutes free, it is

1 7

the shapely and mournful delay she keeps alive for him the breathing

1 8

as the long body of the beach grows emptier awaiting him

1 9

gathering the holocaust in close to its heart growing more beautiful

2 0

under the meaning under the soft hands of its undoing

2 1

saying Goodnight goodnight for now going upstairs

2 2

under the kissing of the minutes under the wanting to go on living

2 3

beginning always beginning the ending as they go to sleep beneath her.

BREAKDANCING

[Teresa: SAINT TERESA OF AVILA]

Staying alive the boy on the screen is doing it,
    the secret nobody knows like a rapture through his limbs,
the secret, *the robot-like succession of joint isolations*
    that simulate a body's reaction to
electric shock.
    This is how it tells itself: pops, ticks, waves and the

float. What
    is poverty for, Mr. Speed, Dr. Cadet, Dr. Rage,
Timex? Don't push me the limbs are whispering, don't push
    'cause I'm close to the edge the footwork is whispering
down onto the sidewalk that won't give in won't go some other
    where while the TV

hums and behind me their breathings, husband, daughter, too slow,
    go in to that other place and come back out
unstained, handfuls at a time, air, air—
    The flag of the greatest democracy on earth
waves in the wind with the sound turned off. The current

rubs through the stars and stripes
    like a muttering passing through a crowd and coming out an
anthem,
    string of words on its search
and destroy
    needing bodies, bodies. . . .
I'm listening to where she must not choke. I'm listening
    to where he must not be betrayed. I'm trying

to hear pity, the idiom. I'm trying to lean into those
    marshes and hear
what comes through clean,
    what comes through changed,
having needed us.
    Oh but you must not fail to eat and sleep Teresa murmurs to
her flock,

 staying alive is the most costly gift you have to offer Him—all the while
                                              watching,
    (whispering Lord, what will you have me
do?) for his corporal
    appearance
in the light of the sixteenth century, in the story that flutters
    blowzy over the body of the land
we must now somehow ram
    the radioactive waste

into. He
    showed himself to her in pieces.
First the fingertips, there in mid-air,
    clotting, floating, held up by the invisible, neither rising
nor falling nor approaching nor lingering, then hands, then a

few days later feet, torso, then arms, each part alone, each part
    free of its argument, then days, then eyes,
then face entire, then days again, then *His*
    most sacred humanity in its risen form
was represented to me

completely. "Don't try
    to hold me in yourself (the air, hissing) but try to hold yourself
in me," Nov 18, 1570. I'm listening to where she must not choke,
    I'm listening to where he must not, must not. . . . Air,

holding a girl in a man's arms now,
        making them look like wind,
what if they can't be returned to you
        the *things* now reaching me—the three

exhalings, hum, blue light, the minutes, the massacres, the strict halflife of
        radioactive isotopes, the shallow
graves, the seventeen rememberable personal
        lies? What if they go only this far, grounding
in me, staying
        alive?
Here is the secret: the end is an animal.
        Here is the secret: the end is an animal growing by

accretion, image by image, vote by
        vote. *No more pain* hums the air,
as the form of things shall have fallen
        from thee, no more pain, just the here and the now, the jackpot, the
watching, minutes exploding like thousands of silver dollars all over your
        face your hands but tenderly, almost tenderly, turning mid-air, gleaming,
so slow, as if it could last,
        frame after frame of nowhere

turning into the living past.

HEADLIGHTS

[NEAR DAWN]

And then, you see, it's the last moment, the last, you can hardly keep
your eyes closed much longer, soon the lights will fizz on, a place will
coalesce (all day, believe it or not) and do you know

that girl, good girl, outside the window there, under the blossoming
magnolia?—
               what is she waiting for, for instance, and is the bus

late?—And then, you see, it's a little less early, someone has turned
the birds up full volume and a wind's trying to
say them

and the room is growing streaked with light like doctors hovering round

—so pale, these who once were boys and girls, going plink, ping, in the
light with their instruments

trying to divide out its tendons, its running striations—
                                 The rind of the thing,

which happens to be a room here with day breaking in it,
peeling away, releasing the young queen the underneath, remorseless,
like the thing in the forest which is not the forest. Jesus!—
who's going to help me get up into this today,
what's going to brighten so terribly in one corner I'll have to rise
if only to extinguish it (what is she doing up so early? what is
she waiting for, on the corner, in the corner)—Dear Doctor:

      dear doctor intertwined
with fire: dear are-you-there: dear *shall I*
find examples,
               rising with whirling motion,

dear *my feelings towards you are.* . . . What is she

for, for instance, Miss Patience, what is she going to keep from

happening, for instance? and then, you see, the last of the headlights

flare up against the wall in here, flare up, increase, and pass,
the bus on the way now, the _____ on the way now
to picking her up
            who's fixing her stocking now
                      who's leaning and smoking now

to keep the waiting alive, the open, the wound she believes in, doctor,

and then you see it's not early anymore, it's about to be
late (there's no in-between), the bus is due, her skirt is
in place again, it will round the corner exactly at x, setting in motion (exactly)
the y, the arousal of time into minutes, it's almost here, it's almost now,
(the river is beginning, the lullaby—seed snared, tip of the
tongue)—

as, weaker, now, the patterns rise against the walls, increase,
and pass,
          and draw the shape of place, and pass,

the shape of the flaw, the prettyness, and pass,

—Oh but there is something here that grows (making a shape) and grows against the walls, its argument expanding, incorporating, there is (here it is)

a story which flares out, opening, against these walls, and does not

pass, increasing does not pass, against the walls, against the blank *henceforth*
                                                                              like a wall,

the first light coming to hold the tree now,

the *holding* all over the tree like a stain that won't take,

the girl walking away around whom the randomness

had gathered, the girl having gathered her stocking up into her hands

and tied that knot, walking away, the one in whom we invest

the whole form looking warily around before she turns the corner.

SELF-PORTRAIT
AS DEMETER AND PERSEPHONE

1

So Look I said this is the burning bush we're in it it has three faces

It's a day's work it's the hand that takes and the other one

The other one the mother the one whose grief is the visible world

a wound she must keep open by beginning and beginning

2

Oh but you have to learn to let her go you said
out into the open field through the waiting the waving grasses
way out to the edge of that drastic field of distinctions
each new possibility molting off the back of the one motion, creation,
until there are so many truths each one its own color
it's a flower the picking of which would open the world
the mouth over the unsaid whispering loves me not loves me

Out alone in the field us watching her from a distance

Can she still find the way are the cracks small enough?

3

Meanwhile up here now this is the knowable
clucking I've been looking for you all day clucking I

will not remember O Lord for it will be taken from me
And the meekness shall be the absence of testimony
the eyes that look neither towards nor away
four jays on the hedgerows four blue-grey-black mutterings
and the miles stretched out to tempt the mind into them
tugging and tugging is it beautiful can she hear us?

4

Underneath she was gone into the fire the absence of the past
to where you pay what you owe then you want to pay more
She took off the waiting she stood before him without nouns
He held her where are the images he said we will destroy them
you are in hell now there is no beginning

the outline is a creature that will blur you will forget him

as for motive that shapeliness let us splinter it let us scatter it

there is no reason for this that's what your body is for

5

She watched the smoke where it began what it left off
What will I recognize it to have been she thought
smoke smoke her fingers her eyes like static all over it
Surely I can find it the point of departure she put her hand in
The birds the beaks of the birds the song the heard song
She reached in what is it begins at the end she thought
Where is the skin of the minutes will it ever come off
She reached in there was no underneath what was this coiling
     over her fingers
She reached in she could go no further she was sealed off

It pushed back against her it was hell she could finally lean
It was the given and it was finally given

or is it, or is it. . . . It was then she remembered

slit   hum   mob   wing of

and you what did you do? For a long time I

6

It was then she remembered and looked the other way

7

Why this sky why this air why these mountains why this sky

8

And what does he ask of you, only to fear Him

9

Where does the air end? Where does the sky begin?
She saw the made grieving above her like a mother or winter
the great gap grieving all form and shadow
heard the god of the place lean down and describe the grief:
and he shall be to thee in stead of a mouth and thou shalt be to him
in stead of God

(why should she come back up why should she begin again)

Look she said I have to go back now if you don't mind waiting
But tell me, those minutes whispering Behold the day shall come
are they confounded or do they begin again from scratch each instant
from scratch from dirt like a confession under unbearable torture?

He said Look this is the burning bush we're in it it has two faces

Neither toward nor away the crack opened she surfaced
Where she surfaced it's all the same it's always been so why try
she felt her mother in her body it was easy not to worry
the light flayed her she was a new woman she could inhabit a shape
Minutes go in Words come out A machine for waiting

The first thing she saw when she surfaced was the wind
wrapping like a body round the stiff stripped trees
that would bend more deeply into that love if they could
to accompany its eagerness young wind its rage
if they weren't so perfect if they weren't so shorn

(the tinfoil winking in the snowmelt the rinds)

that would bend more deeply into it inventing (if they could)

1 5

another body, exploded, all leafiness, unimaginable

1 6

by which to be forgiven by which to suffer completely this wind

THE LOVERS

They have been staring at each other for a long time now.
Around them the objects (circa 1980).
Then corridors, windows, a meadow, the _____.
They have been staring at the end of each other for a long
time now.
She tries to remember but it is hopeless.
She tries the other one—Hope—casting outward
        a bit,
oh but it costs too much.
Either they're coming for us now or they're not says Love.
Around them objects, minutes, *No* said quickly in passing.
Here it is, *here*, the end of beauty, the present.
What the vista fed into. What it wants to grow out of, creeping,
        succulent. . . .
No No says the voice pinpointing the heart of these
        narrows.
Draw draw the curtain now.
You there in your seat, you there.
Here is the glance, between them, quick, the burning.
Here is the glance afloat—on the back of what, dear nothingness?
Here it is, here—
They've decided they'll feed everything into it and then they'll see.
They've decided they want the rest tight round them now like
        this.
They want to be owned, it is all that can own them.
The look, the look finally free of the anything looked-for,
the hurry finally come unstuck of the hurrying,

something fiery all around like dust or a jury.
You there. They are done talking.
They are done waiting.
Either they are or they're not, she thinks, hold still.
Something fiery all round—let it
        decide.
It will need us to shape it (won't it?)   hold still.
And the cries increasingly   hold still.
Like a _____ this look between us   hold still.
If, inside, a small terrified happiness begins
like an idea of color
like an idea of color sinking to stain an instance, a *thing*,
like an arm holding a lit candle in a door that is parting,
if, oh if—banish it.
Listen, this is the thing that can trap it now—the glance—
the howling and biting gap—
and our two faces raised
that nothing begin (don't look away),
that there be no elsewhere,
that there be no elsewhere to seed out into,
just this here between us, this look (can you see me?) this
        look afloat on want,
this long thin angel whose body is a stalk, rootfree,
        blossomfree,
whose body we are making, whose body is a _____,
(only quicker, much quicker, a conflagration)
an angel, the last one, the only one that can still live
        here
(while out in the corridor they are taking down names)
(while out in the corridor the shoes purr for the blacking)
the last one, the very last,
alive, yes—yes—but wingless this *between*, wingless—

VERTIGO

Then they came to the very edge of the cliff and looked down.
Below a real world flowed in its parts, green, green.
The two elements touched—rock, air.
She thought of where the mind opened out
into the sheer drop of its intelligence,
the updrafting pastures of the vertical in which a bird now rose,
blue body the blue wind was knifing upward
faster than it could naturally rise,
up into the downdraft until it was frozen until she could see them
                                                            at last
the stages of flight, broken down, broken free,
each wingflap folding, each splay of the feather-sets flattening
for entry.... *Parts* she thought, *free* parts, watching the laws
at work, *through which desire must course*
seeking an ending, seeking a shape. Until the laws of flight and fall
                                                            increased.
Until they made, all of an instant, a bird, a blue
enchantment of properties no longer
knowable. What is it to understand, she let fly,
leaning outward from the edge now that the others had gone down.
How close can the two worlds get, the movement from one to the other
being death? She tried to remember from the other life
the passage of the rising notes off the violin
into the air, thin air, chopping their way in,
wanting to live forever—marrying, marrying—yet still free of the
                                                            orchestral swelling
which would at any moment pick them up, in-

corporate. How is it one soul wants to be owned
by a single other
in its entirety?—
What is it sucks one down, offering itself, only itself, for
ever? She saw the cattle below
moving in a shape which was exactly their hunger.
She saw—could they be men?—the plot. She leaned. How does one enter
a story? Where the cliff and air pressed the end of each other,
everything else in the world—woods, fields, stream, start of another
                                        darker

woods—appeared as kinds of
falling. She listened for the wind again. What was it in there
                            she could hear
that has nothing to do with *telling the truth*?
What was it that was *not her listening*?
She leaned out. What is it pulls at one, she wondered,
what? That it has no shape but point of view?
That it cannot move to hold us?
Oh it has vibrancy, she thought, this emptiness, this intake just
                            prior to
the start of a story, the mind trying to fasten
and fasten, the mind feeling it like a sickness this wanting
to snag, catch hold, begin, the mind crawling out to the edge of the cliff
and feeling the body as if for the first time—how it cannot
follow, cannot love.

RAVEL AND UNRAVEL

So that it's right, isn't it, that she should come to love it best,
the unraveling, every night,
the hills and cypresses turning back
into thread, then patience again, then . . .
is it emptiness?
All the work of the eyes and breath and fingertips that forced
     the three dimensions down
into each other going now, all of an instant, back
to what other
place?
Because we were lost, taking our time, today,
taking the long way back
from looking for the Indian petroglyphs we knew were there
but couldn't find, alone in the miles, the wind
kissing the rocks
to translate them down.
You walked ahead, navigating, lost one, carrying
Emily, all cargo now that I
am emptied finally
of all but my own
undoing
like the sun rising over these gigantic rock formations
coming to touch, in time, every millimeter
of every declivity, rounding, pronouncing them
into the emptiness.
So that I don't know if the cry was one I heard or
realized, clinging to the windy unsaid as it did,

hovering in, and diving madly from, the possible, the poverty,
wild, high-pitched, mewing and hissing and
knifing down
from two young eagles
into the heart.
They dove they rose,
as helpless on the draft as in control.
Was it the sky's? Was it my listening silting in?
It was the cry where play and kill are one.
It made me hear how clean the sky around them was of
anything I might have trapped it with.
So when I heard her crying up ahead,
pulling me in,
I heard her cry not add itself
to this enclosure of an emptiness
growing more empty as the minutes flick. I heard
how it stood for strength and was not of that strength.
Unlike that screech, that ancient breath
with a shape above me,
it was desire.
I could hear how she and her cry went separate ways,
one to be lost, one to be wholly
found out, word for word, taking the place of the sky.
Because there is a moment which is the mother. It flicks
open, alive,
here and *here* though here she's
clothed she's
already gone, only siren, kingdom without extension,
secret sexual place of
placelessness.
Her body opens, burns,
at the edge of each rock each cliff
where the dust is pulling free,

wild in the air again
momentarily,
all arms, the light touching round each mote, each grain, alive, more than
alive. . . .
Then the beautiful, the view all round us, with that crimp of use in it,
then the husband minutes bearing down, bearing down—

P I E T À

—Then the sunshine striking all sides of his body but only
in pieces, in bits—the torso torn from the back, from the arm
that falls back, then three
fingers ripped up by the light into view,

then the lifted knee taken up, taken back, then the ankle, the back of

the head—Like an explosion that will not end
this dismemberment which is her lifting him up, dismemberment
of flesh into minutes. Are they notes, these parts, what is the
song, can you hear it, does it sound beautiful and true to the one

on the other side who hears it all at

once, cadenza of gaps? When she still had him in her,
unseen, unbroken, what did she have?
Before she gets him back there is something he has to cross,
as god, as thief, something he has to marry—Meanwhile

to his left the linen garment he has discarded

is held up by five soldiers
bartering for it, blazing where the light snags on the delicate
embroidery, and black where the neck-hole gapes, black
where the body is seen to be

missing, the form

gone. The five boys bid on it, chance holds it up in the slight wind
and takes their coins for it, this souvenir of the world murmuring
nothing nothing which sounds like God
hast Thou forsaken

me, a small cry fed onto the back of the breeze, small

among the dusksounds, among the opening cries of the early
nightfeeders, small metered cry the breeze takes in among the prey cries,
among the price cries. Listen. Do you hear it at
last, the spirit of

matter, there, where the words end—their small heat—where the details

cease, the scene dissolves, do you feel it at last, the sinking, where the
                                                  meaning
rises, where the meaning evaporates, into history, into the day the
mind, and the precipitating syllables are free at last
on the wind, sinking, the proof of god the cry sinking to where it's

just sound, part of one sound, one endless sound—maybe a cry maybe a

countdown, love—

ROOM TONE

Turn around (wind in the sycamore).
Did you see that did you hear that (wind in the
_____ _____ _____?) can you touch it,
what *can* you touch? will you
speak back to me,
will you look up now, please?
Dear reader, is it enough for you that I am thinking of you
in this generic sort of way,
moving across the page for you that your eyes move,
moving in and out of these rooms that there be a *there*
for you?
Is it less fearful that you are held *in mind*
even if only as an instance?
Can you pray to it?
Can you give yourself over?
Whereupon these syllables raise up like new seed, talk, talk,
and the war ends,
and the sounds go back into the noise like boys who survived
re-entering the wheat fields now. . . .
Consider this: there was a room neither you nor I are in nor can we
be.
Here it is: the light was so white you had to push to see.
To see the limbs in it, the instances.
The white metal chair against the whitewashed walls.
The white stone floor.
A jacket (mine?) white linen hanging on a nail.
A thistle in a coffee

can. Turn around—
did you can you will you (a letter unopened) (a knife
in the sink). A time of year laying itself onto the windowsill
should we want to touch it.
The unseen up for grabs.
Here it is: even a fly made an important shadow.
And here: the place most like *life* in the pleats, in the knife's under-
side.
When the man in it held the woman in it they knew as if
for the first time and all of an instant that. . . .
And flatly. Wasting no time.
When he held her down as if groundcover
they came as close as one can.
Like the gloss of the thing and the thing.
No room to turn around in.
Fallen down, there, for all the world to see.
Lingering and merciless and without knowledge.
The two of them, for that instant, of the world,
the knot where the millions of souls collect and crawl.
And no room to turn in.
And no wonder at all.
The American moment.
Golden one golden one.
Higher than justice, no one watching, no eyes at all
on them, let's say,
as if at the bottom of some mind and irretrievable,
and then, then—
let's say the date crept in over the windowsill,
an *important* date,
saying excuse me are you there may I leave
a message?
Then the sound of a wagonwheel in the street,
a man calling out names and prices,

then the children running alongside the donkey kicking it
and a smell called *blue*—
What you have to get, friend, is the room after they've
just left it.
They will never be together again death will intervene.
They will not touch each other again who own each other.
Nothing will be good thereafter.
(Cataracts, kidney disease, a stroke in the month of May)
(No money and, after a while—et cetera)
Sinking, sinking, that moment, to the bottom of the mind,
into the narrative (So saying her rash hand in evil hour—)
into manifest destiny (Thus to herself she pleasingly began—)
Until it is now. Until *this is what you want to do now, reader*:
you want to get it back,
you want to hear it, in here now, the background, *room tone*,
the thing ticking behind this voicetrack,
the thing you can't dance to,
listen—
what clicks beneath this talk,
beneath the hissing of the storyline slipping her dress off
(closing her mouth almost too suddenly as she unfastens)
(are you watching?) (are you?)
(and then on the fortieth morning they—)
(and then on the fortyfifth morning they—)
and it has to be noise or you're not getting it,
something into which your listening
cannot disappear,
as in, here they are *in each other*,
and here is the daylight now, look,
and this a lifted hand up into it,
and a name repeated slowly to indicate _____,
and here the one (half-cup of?) breath being exchanged by the two
                                                        bodies,

the one breath back and forth and back and forth until they're dizzy they're
making themselves sick, in the white room, in the
(as in the land of darkness yet in light) white room, so white,
(and fansie that they feel
divinitie within them breeding wings) how white? (wherewith to scorn
the earth)
and freedom (click) and minutes (click) and
(under amazement of their hideous change)
something like what's called *being-born* (click, click

ANNUNCIATION

She's not sure she can hear it outside of the daylight,
the small sound of matter wanting to be changed,
she's not sure she can hear it outside of the daylight,
the small sound of matter wanting to be changed into minutes,
outside of the lie, the small click where silence slaps
against that gear (chain saw?), that trill(?),
outside of *outside* where the voice downtown announces
over the p.a. the race's arrivals one by one,
the numbers called out by lungs onto the small
harbor winds, onto the trucks-eight-miles-away-hitting-the-upgrade-on-50. . . .
She's not sure she can, listening into the slippery leaping
of one thing into another
for *shape* which is a faltering where it suddenly ceases
to falter (for a *reason*, is that important?)
close by that trill again and the splash where three birds I
had altogether missed hit the leaves is that
important, not a fullness yet, not a sentence yet, but a thinning,
a suggestion of distance in the flat, as where the
minute before and the minute before, like so many souls
the *under* keeps feeding forth feeding forth, cease.

*

If she turns she'll see them already,
the neighbors on their roofs, sunbathing, very still,
like nouns one by one on their striped towels,
two down on the lawn—

From one point of view you could count
their turns, watching the row of bodies
revolve, diminish.

You could look down over the alphabet
and watch the motives blossom.

Here is what is rising in the bodies (that you
cannot see), rising, as if from a long way off,
like a nourishment along a runner and stalk you
cannot see, no:
a fatigue; a desire—like a murmur that will not
cease—to be taken up;
a small calculation in the soul involving a trade,
a *take this from me but give me give*
me . . . ; a wish to be chosen; a wish to be
spared; a slippage in the soul there under
the hot sun, under the stillness, the dark glasses, the
waiting, a slippage, a downshifting of waiting
into patience, of patience into pattern (the light,
remember?), of pattern into
beauty. . . . *What is the difference*
between being spared and being saved whispers
the light without shadow over the row of still
bodies, splaying itself down them,
running up and down them unseen, unfelt,
dividing itself into their parts,
rushing back into itself above them,
slipping and pooling and shattering and regrouping this
light no shadow splices—

Here is what rises up from their waiting
into the light that cannot seize them: desire:
desire that is not heat into heat that is not desire.

See this: the heat playing over the desire.

All day waiting, all day turning into the
turning, the sun the rays the great rhetorician,

down over the shoulders as if for meaning over the shore,

darkening the shoulders, there, in the awful music of
coincidence.

*

Later the wind will come up, friends
will drop by, there will be a cookout in the
back around dusk.

The earth the mother of the dead will seep up
into them: laughter, some stories and dance.

The giant body of meaning will fold their
four hundred sixty-seven actions in, adding and dividing: shape.

Like a thought it will close by beginning another,
endless unbearable corridor: fate.

Outside the last birds twittering and the long slow coos and
hoots of the night-feeders.

The room is empty now: this is where they sat,
this is where they turned, first saw the . . . .

But now when she presses her face down onto the grass,
down, further, the hot sun upon her, pushing,
she smells the dilution of a great
blunt smell into the endless blades, and looking up

sees miles and miles of it, smells the
thinness of it, the great expenditure of it
into the endless instances. Even
pushing, even face down, even into it where it's thick, there, in the
reeds, the drainage, wet, she smells the dilution, the small
allotment. By which I am spared? she
thinks, outline and syllable? By which the
whole is not dismembered but thinned,
elaborated, exemplified? By which I am
spared she thinks or is it, or is it . . . pressing her face down
into the instances—

POLLOCK AND CANVAS

PART I

When he leaned down over
    the undefeated soil
to make it end somewhere,
    to make it beautiful
(go nowe forthe, thou litel songe upon
    my message), when

he leaned down through the space
    which separated him from it,
down through the way and the life,
    and the garment of minutes (and sey that I
give hir) and the garment of light (hert body and
    minde) parting the past from the future with his leaning,
a flare, a tiny quick
    freedom (let no waves

let no winde, let no stormes, let not the salte
    see . . .), what he chose—can you understand
this—what he chose (go forthe
    in hast)
what he chose
    through the see-no-evil, through the eye for
the eye,
    choosing to no longer let the brushtip touch,
at any point,
    the still ground,

was to not be trans-
    formed but to linger
in the hollow, the about-to-be whispering *Yes*
    I understand you whispering
tell me then what will render
    the body alive? whispering (leaning down
further) *is there anything finally opposite*
    to life? (his brush

hovering, his brush able to cut a figure
    on the blank and refusing) whispering *suppose the imperishable* . . .
whispering *may not the same be said for,*
    the leaning out itself a kind of whispering. . . .
The king can neither ride nor walk, neither lie nor stand, he
    leans but cannot sit and sighs
remembering. There is a lake called

    _____. There is a ritual silver bowl
    found at _____ in a bog.
On the outside deities, unidentified, and within
    a series
of scenes. . . . There is a lake, they bring him there for the
    air for his painful open wound, he calls it his
hunting day, what can he catch there with his wound so painful
    that would provision
his home?

PART II

1

Here is the lake, the open, he calls it his day; fishing.

The lake, the middle movement, woman's flesh, maya.

And here is the hook before it has landed, before it's deep in the current,

the hovering—keeping the hands off—the gap alive,

the body of talk between the start and beauty,

all limbs this one sucked alive by delay and brought to stand here in the room among the rest of the forms

this girl all accident all *instead-of*, of the graces the

most violent one, the one all gash, all description,

(between the creator and the created: a flash: a girl)

10

(the most violent one) (*one cannot produce depth only the sensation of dep*

11

(without embarrassment, without shame) the most violent one—

12

as in *I can* (the hook hissing mid-air) *control the flow of paint, there is no accident no beginning no end. . . .*

13

Oh but we wanted to paint what is not beauty, how can one paint what is not beauty . . . ?

14

And I will cover thee with my hand when I pass by

15

And will take away my hand and thou shalt see my back my

16

form—The most violent one, standing there with her hand on her hip, gorgeo gap between the mind and the world, water, water,

17

the line being fed out the line without shape before it lands without death

18

saying a good life is possible, still hissing, still unposited,

19

before it lands, without shape, without generation, or form that bright fruit
(a part of the place but cut out from the place)—

20

not in the wanting,

21

not motionless but not in the wanting yet, the image,

22

the unsaid billowing round the hook, updrafting, caressing,

23

the light whispering never (can you hear it?) have we been here

24

before can you hear it never never green hook in the sunny

25

day, young, beginning to sink,

2 6

down through the day the netting of chance her body

2 7

as the young god stole down through the suffering to come up with a meaning
form

2 8

which is nothing more than a desire for clearly matched theft and punishmen

2 9

and the streames of hir heavenly looke shall all your sorrows
steer

3 0

and down into the end finally still on the ground there beneath him.

PART III

Where does the end
    begin?
where does the lifting off of hands become
    love,
letting the made wade out into danger,
    letting the form slur out into flaw, in-

conclusiveness? Where does the end of love

begin? (Where does *that* love begin?)
    And then He rested, is that where the real
making
    begins—the now—Then He rested letting in chance letting in
any wind any shadow quick with minutes, and whimsy,
    through the light, letting the snake the turning
in. Then things not yet true
    which slip in

are true,
    aren't they?
Where is the border of *stopping* and *ending*?
    And the land was waste but the king did not die,
his brother died but something king did not die,
    molting,
not at any point
    dead.

    The clouds *like transcripts* over the pond
(did not die), the grammar the deepwater which mutters
    long before the sentence (hissing, mid-air)
begins
    and keeps on keeps on, under the caught fish, lifted, silvery,
keeping the wound
    alive. The caught with its outline, promising, promising. . . .
It is the window that makes things difficult (but here

there is no window) it is
the eyes that cannot see *the present*
    that flit, naming, with a carpenter's
lateness.
    The exterior of x is the body. . . .
The exterior of stopping is ending. . . .
    Look down here into this open sepulcher

(unstretched) what has he planted? What's coming up?
     Is it a shape a dead thing?
We used to think that shape, a finished thing, was a corpse
     that would sprout—Easter in every heart—what do we
think

now?
     What we want is to paint nothing how can one paint nothing?
The look of spontaneity
     comes up, the figure. Has it a name? Can you nail it?
—arms, eyes, is it a woman is it three women moving towards
     one man, is it what we did and why
why
     this girl this girl

rising in the mind in place of the mind,
     shedding her garment like a sense of earlyness, shedding the next one
as the possible slips off the shoulders of the true,
     bright shoulders rising up (birdscreech, daybreak) likewise the next one
and the next, shedding your hands on her,
     your wish, altogether, shedding your eyes on her,

sticky, as petals drop off, all at once, just after rain, just as the
     first light strikes,
and the meaning of the rose rises up,
     (shedding the meaning of the rose)
and the memory of the rose rises up
     (shedding the memory of the rose)—

(the hands lifting off, the mind lifting off, the wish lifting off, all
     at once now)

Oh she would be a readyness, a first clearing, a sound
     beginning at the end of sound, an escape from,

escape from. . . . But can she step free into
    that chapel say I
do, can the girl come clean of the mother's body,
    the legs are still up there where does she end,
you can't pick her out can't choose a thing here—
    what's the title, the scales won't wash off,
the shimmering scales won't and she

stand up clean on the shore and walk towards you, no,
    —A shell, he said, a nut, a plum, a pear, a
kidney a carrot a treetrunk he said a bird a
    bird a lark a shore a bulrush he said a
mountain a bone—(is it enough will it provision his home?)

        . . . . . The moment
    a figure appears on the canvas, she said,
the story begins, the story begins the error sets in,
    the error the boredom, she said, the story talking louder
than the paint, she said, the boredom the hurry, she said
    (without embarrassment, without shame)
(and you must learn to feel shape as simply shape whispered the
    wind, not as description not as reminiscence not as what

it will become)
    (down past the birds the daybreak the glass
in the landfill glimmering, reminding) (down past the blind girl on our corner now
    turning to face the wind, waiting for the light
to change)
    (and I will take away mine hand, He said,

and I will take away mine hand and thou, thou. . . .)

EVENING PRAYER

Someone has cut the grass. Someone has cut your tall
    new grass, the sweetness
smears a wild raw dress onto the air, and she
is rising, turning now,
                    in sun, in wind, and she

is free. . . . Walking home
I saw the shadow of a bird, like a heart, like a scythe.
I saw the shadow-wings cross through a wall.

The vacant-lot weeds, too, swayed there. And thistles,
    pods. Terrible
silky wall, abandoned warehouse, thigh. . . .
And the elms, burnt now, were young
all over it, and the wind

in its fatigue. . . .
             But the bird, fistful of time and sinew, blue,
dragged down over the cinderblock by light, lawed down and
brushstroked down—how he went through, went
    abstract,
clean. Not hungry there and not afraid. Thou shalt

dash it to pieces, then, Hand-in-the-light, this potter's
    vessel, vast atomic
girl, shall clean it further, further, spill
    the hollow from her, know her?

OF FORCED SIGHTES
AND TRUSTY FEREFULNESS

Stopless wind, here are the columbine seeds I have
collected. What we would do with them is
different. Though both your trick and mine flowers blue
and white

with four stem tails and yellow underpetals. Stopless
and unessential, half-hiss, half-
lullaby, if I fell in among your laws,
if I fell down into your mind your snow, into the miles

of spirit-drafts you drive, frenetic multitudes,
out from timber to the open ground and back to no
avail, if I fell down, warmblooded, ill, into your endless
evenness,

into this race you start them on and will not let them win . . . ?
If I fell in?
What is your law to my law, unhurried hurrying?
At my remove from you, today, in your supremest

calculation, re-
adjustment, are these three birds scratching for dead
bark beetles, frozen seeds, too late for being here yet only
        here,
in the stenchfree

cold. This is another current, river of rivers, this thrilling
third-act love. Who wouldn't want to stay
behind? They pack the rinds away, the blazing applecores,
the frantic shadow-wings scribbling the fenceposts, window-

panes. Meanwhile you turn, white jury, draft, away,
deep justice done.
I don't presume to cross the distances, the clarity,
but what grows in your only open hands? Or is

digressive love,
row after perfect greenhouse row,
the garden you're out of for good, wind of the theorems,
of proof, square root of light,

chaos of truth,
blinder than the mice that wait you out
    in any crack?
This is the best I can do now for prayer—to you,
for you—these scraps I throw

my lonely acrobats
that fall
of your accord
right to my windowsill: they pack it away, the grains, the

accidents, they pack it deep into the rent
heart of the blue
spruce, skins in with spiky needles. . . . Oh
    hollow
charged with forgetfulness,

through wind, through winter nights, we'll pass,
steering with crumbs, with words,
making of every hour
a thought, remembering

by pain and rhyme and arabesques of foraging
the formula for theft
under your sky that keeps
sliding away

married to hurry
and grim song.

IMPERIALISM

Nothing but a shadow, lord, and hazy at that, at my feet,
    that not even the dust and the gravel can hold.
And when a bird-call happens
    can it (anywhere) intersect with the shadow or the gravel or the
voice stuttering somewhere above it *foxglove blooms* and then
    wind blows to bend the foxglove all one way?

I can see the wind in the hair of the shadow.
    I can see its sleeve flutter from torn to whole and back
in a flash.
    Now it coats a bank of stonecrop, a butterfly, a hole where a rock
someone lifted is
    missing,

now it returns them to the sun, unchanged.
    What I want to know, dear are-you-there,
is what it *is*, this life a shadow and a dust-road have,
    the shape constantly laying herself down over the sparkling dust
she cannot own—
    What can they touch of one another, and what is it for

this marriage, this life of Look, here's a body, now here's
    a body, now here,
here. . . .
    Last night I watched your face in the lamplight fluttering—
We were trying to talk—The kerosene was thinning—

You never had your face but something like cleared light then
        soiled light
(roiling)
        and on it all—imprint that would not take—eyeholes, mouth
hole. There were moths.
        There were foodstains my fingers found in the woodgrain.
Later there were cruelties exchanged
        between us.
Once you stood up grabbed your hat put it back down.
        When you sat down again we were not free.

There was a space across which you and your shadow, pacing,
        broke,
and around you pockets of shadow, sucking, shutting.
        By now the talk had changed.
There was a liquid of wall and stove and space-behind-the-stove.
        And x where the mirror had been.
And x where the window had been.
        And x where my hand slid over the tabletop breaking a glass.

There were shadows in the shadows, and in there were cuts.

        It took all that we are
to keep the thing clear—the narrative of
        bentwood chair and hinge and trim where the linoleum
grips. . . .
        We sat in the one world and let her seep on into us, old hag,
all holes—
        What would she be
without us

willing to sit and clarify and try to nail

it shut? We give her that glitzy fluttering, her body, by the one deep-driven
        nail of point-of-view,
don't we? And there was a story I wanted
        to tell you then but couldn't
(just where she came on into us and we pushed back with
        better rephrasings) (dear Cinderella) (dear Cinderella our shut eyes re.

to ash) there was a story
        about how as a child Mother took me to see
the great river Ganges
        in the Imperial city of Calcutta. Dear secret,
what was it I saw?
        On the one bank (our bank)
bodies crushed, teeming, washing their knives, themselves, their sick,
        and linens, and dishes, and newborn
calves —— tens and hundreds of thousands of bodies mostly
        wet and partly naked even now pressing to get to
waterfront

in a hot sun the river thou shalt not step into twice dear god
        utensils and genitalia and incandescent linens —(I was nine)—.
Not far upriver were the pyres, and because she wished for me
        to *know the world*
we had watched a number of bodies (of burnings) that morning

then watched the pulleys lift
        the fine-meshed grille covered with ash and cartilage
down into the river
        and shake it, and shake it (at the end of its chains).
It was near noon. I watched its pattern which told a story
        in metal and held a tree and heaven and 2 animals

beside the naked woman's shape
    shudder in the river as if to imprint it
and then submerge (no trace) then rise back up
    and something like a tree and haunches reappear
on the face of the waters.
    Later she had me walk on in.
Strange water. Thick. I can recall it even now. The more
    it slipped off you the more it clung to you
and caked

so that the only sense of cleanliness you got
    was in the decision
to stop
    and let the sun reclaim you, and let it seal the film of silt
down tight.
    Of course we showered in the hotel.
Why does this matter now?
    I know I didn't even touch that place. That it's *exotic*

even now, and here, whatever imagery might
    be of use. What is the usery that's deep enough?
The story goes I cried so much in the hotel that night
    they had to call whatever doctor was on hand
to give me a shot of what? — probably Demerol —
    to stop the screaming. She
tried to hold me to her, I'm sure,

making it worse,
    since her body (in particular) was
no longer relevant. I remember
    looking up out of the water
and seeing that the other bank although quite far away
    was visible

and utterly blank—
        —not one face, rock, tree, hut, road, tent, sign—
just haze and flat—a line drawn simply to finish

the river, to make that motion *seem a river*—
        There must have been trees—no? sacred cows?
I looked up nine years of age soaking wet,
        the bodies of all those strangers against me—
(you can't tip forward, you have to sink down)—
        and over there seeing it, whatever it was,

like a held breath over there, like a mouth held agape with
        hesitation? delay? like a listening that has just ceased
over there. . . .
        Of course I know, since, there are reasons
it remain so uninhabited, that bank, I know since it's
        a law—But what I remembered last night to tell you

is a white umbrella a man in the river near me was washing
        and how the dark brown ash-thick riverwater rode
in the delicate tines as he raised it rinsing.
        How he opened it and shut it. Opened and shut it.
First near the surface then underwater—

—*first near the surface then underwater*—
        And as for her body ("no longer relevant")
it became nothing to me after that, or something less,
        because I saw what it was, her body, you see—a line
brought round, all the way round, reader, a plot, a
        shape, one of the finished things, one of the

beauties (hear it click shut?) a thing

completely narrowed down to love—all arms, all arms extended in the
    pulsing sticky heat, fan on, overhead on, all
arms no face at all dear god, all arms—